STFM

Afterword Press

ISBN: 978-1-952555-05-3

STFM

Find
Still Trying to Forgive Myself
Free

By

QED Jones

Table of Contents

A Lone Wolf's Love Story Pt. 1

Every wolf that lives past adolescence knows 2 things,

The way to survive on its own

And that it was never meant to do so.

How ironic,

Mastering a skill while hoping to never use it

Because implementation leads to death.

This is how I came to know writing.

An art dressed in oppression,

A curse wrapped in eventually.

But despite what we've been taught,

Nightmares will always be met,

And lone wolves are more common than we thought.

Pen2Pad

They say the best way to become a writer is to write.

Build up a habit of practicing.

So what does it say about me that the only writing habit I ever picked up was never writing down any of the things I really needed to say?

I wish I could remember the first poem I didn't write.

Was it the day I'd had?

Or the poem itself that kept me quiet?

Did I tell myself I'd be more creative in the morning?

Or pray that I'd mistake my gift for a half-remembered dream?

I wonder if that was the day I confused silence for self-care.

I wonder if by then I was already too comfortable with my despair.

I wonder if it was about my father...

I bet it was.

I used to write about him often.

I hope there were jokes in it,

Or maybe a funny story.

A simile I could use today,

Or a metaphor that doesn't bore me.

But I know better than that.

The first one is like the hundreds that followed,

A camera roll of all the disappointments that I hid in the stillness of a picture.

But if you're reading this,

I'm finally going through my old photos.

Beach House

The game begins with describing a house.

No other instructions,

Just close your eyes and describe what comes to mind.

I saw the blue first...

Only a shade darker than the water it was next to,

I'm home here.

The house is wide and tall,

2 stories.

Plus an attic and a basement,

I can never be high enough to escape the fear of what I keep

hidden below.

It has 3 bedrooms.

I need to pretend I'll invite people here,

That's probably why there's music playing.

The living room is my favorite.

Its wall is a window that faces the water,

And when the tide rises they meet just beyond my toes.

I know I stay here.

No one else is welcome.

Afterwards they tell me the house is me in the way I think I'm

perceived,

I wonder if that's why I never saw a door.

The Struggle is Real

There once was a cage that brought forth a song,
Of a bird who used to fly on winds long gone.
Now that same cage is keeping me from the one I love,
But has forced me to appreciate her details like when hand meets glove.

So which is more beautiful when all is said and done?
The freedom?
Or the harmonious cries for it that this cage has given everyone?

Talk2God

The first time I stopped praying, it was a suicide attempt.
I hoped that if God could forget my voice,
Then taking my breath would be the logical next step.
I figured it'd be easier for people to mourn if they couldn't blame themselves.

The second time I stopped praying, it was out of frustration.
God was only answering me in the poems I hadn't written,
And I didn't appreciate the irony.
I'm still learning to fully love my craft.

Check the Roots

At the funeral, I promised his mother that I'd watch after his little brother.

Last week, I saw him on the train for the 1st time in years,

He didn't even recognize me.

I never saw the family resemblance in promises and punishment.

Never realized how often a swing and a miss can turn into a shackle,

Or a brand,

Or the final guess in a game of hangman.

I blame myself so easily.

Taught myself to carry so much.

I wonder if this is how Peter forgot how to fly?

Siren Song Pt. 1

When I was younger,
I could close my eyes and tell the difference
Between a police car and a fire truck just by the sound of the sirens.
Years later, I stared into the face of an angel
And somehow managed to mistake her voice for the screech of a
Siren's song.
That was the first time life tried to caution me about using skills
learned in trauma on the days I'm seeking peace.

Therapeutic

`

For a time, I was angry.
I believed there was a plan,
I just couldn't find its course.

For a moment, I was content.
I believed there was a plan,
I just had to stay the course.

For a future, I was humbled.
I believed there was a plan,
I just had to be grateful it expanded the course.

A List of Things I Observed While the TV Was Supposed to Rot My Brain

1. On October 19th, 1994, the series finale of the TV show Dinosaurs aired. In its final scene, the father looks into the eyes of his wife and children and apologizes for allowing his infatuation with technology to make him forget about nature's beauty and eventually bringing on the apocalypse. Somehow 2020 still managed to end up feeling like a prequel to iRobot. I guess history is more wheeled then this timeline.

2. I started Lost 2 years after the finale and nobody told me nothing. I host friendship Olympics every other year now.

3. Whenever I get too caught up in thinking about my legacy, I remember that the Lost Boys never even mourned Rufio.

4. The world still don't give a damn about how sensitive we Black boys are, but I'm hoping we can start to care for each other more.

5. The Manifesto of Plays with Squirrels.

5. The day I figured out how Shaun knew Feeny's retirement party was the last time he'd see Angela is the day I realized that love is a verb and I was all nouns. Or predicates. Or metaphors. Like the 1st drop of rain that hits after you checked the forecast but thought you had enough time to make it back.

5. When the tension between life and lessons climaxes in a valley, I wonder who thinks they failed more. The mentor or the mentee?

6. It always made sense to me that the Midnight Society reused villains. I've mastered dressing up the same excuses to explain why every time you come to visit I'm still running in place.

7. I'm still confused that it took adulthood for me to realize Joker makes more sense than anyone else in Gotham.

8. In the original stories, the Tin Man was a human. After a curse is placed on him, his entire body is replaced with tin except for his heart which made him unable to love the woman he intended to marry. His entire journey with Dorothy is then based on the memory of a feeling. Sounds like an addict to me.

9. My favorite Disney song is an interlude. The one where Aladdin boldly states that's there's more to him than meets the eye before he hides it from everyone he loves because the best secrets are the ones that you aren't sure exist.

10. Mary Poppins kept her whole world in that suitcase. I'm still hoping that one day, something good will come from my baggage.

Photosynthesis

They told us that flowers need the sun to grow,
But never bother to acknowledge the ones that grew because they knew they needed sun.
I watched a rose crack through the concrete that it never asked to be born beneath,
Simply to fulfill its purpose of blooming,
Simply to be.
Oh, how it contemplated staying in the dark.
Accepting that its present was better than its purpose,
Convinced by the sounds of life above that it wasn't needed,
Wasn't missed.
So determined to be silent so as to not disrupt the routine of others,
Valuing the peace of the piece of the world that it was so sure would never value it,
Because why would they?
They've been fine this long without its presence,
So beneath it sat.
And above I waited.
Oh, how the world sang when we finally met.

<u>Insights</u>

If asked to describe myself,

I'd tell you that I believe both that everyone needs therapy

And that going to see a therapist is a scam.

And if that doesn't make sense to you,

Then know that I've decided it's unlikely we will be friends.

If asked to be honest,

I'd tell you that I remember both the day I built a wall around my heart

And the day that I thought I tore it down.

And that growing up has meant figuring out which one was actually

traumatic.

If asked to tell a story,

I'd tell you that my favorites are both about me

And about nothing at all.

And that if you find the right metaphor,

Nothing about this beginning will surprise you.

A Lone Wolf's Love Story Pt. 2

A lone wolf joining a new pack is nothing short of chaotic.

It comes to breed,

And thus to lead.

The former alpha is either driven out,

Or beaten into submission.

The entire family order shifts.

They must unlearn and relearn how to follow.

Their interactions will adjust.

Everything depends on this realignment.

Growth, I've learned, is like an earthquake.

Inevitable.

Invisible.

You do all you can to prepare,

But when it happens, all you can do is hope your foundation is ready to

be this close to the faults.

Nights Like This

Some nights, I lay awake and think
About the ocean of tears my bloodline held back to make sure we
stayed strong.
Just for me to have the freedom
To cry about how strong we had to always be
As I learn about what that strength cost us.

Grown Folks Business

As a child, I overheard a man say,

"You'll never stop lying to yourself,

Until you find a lie worth telling the truth about."

I always wondered what he meant,

And why he said it into the nothing.

Yesterday I pronounced my love,

To the memory of a woman I'd said I didn't care about,

Through a window as black as the dawn because I couldn't stand my reflection.

I remembered the old man,

And why my mother always told me to stay out of grown folks business.

Blame it on the Boogie

They say the boogie man is just a neglected imaginary friend,

Lurking in the dark to bring nightmares where there should have been attention.

But in these parts, nightmares are all too often safer than reality,

So in reality the boogie is a better friend than I ever thought could have been imagined.

Call him a bad influence.

The conductor on the train to the bad path with me.

Who else is gonna help me grow up too fast?

The trouble with finding the scapegoat is you never know what to do when you catch it.

But don't listen to me,

Only kids believe in the boogie man.

Who Knows

Legend has it that every time a child is born a person dies.

Well, I hope they're wrong.

I've done enough bad on my own without adding murder to my catalog.

Lied, cheated, stole

Something different for every watch I own.

I think in another life I was maybe something great,

But this version of me is getting all the blessings by mistake.

Maybe I was a gracious king,

Ruling with kindness and respect.

A leader of the people,

Who the history books forgot.

Or perhaps the heavens just have yet to lose hope in me.

Maybe I'm too hard on myself,

Maybe God sees something more in me,

And all I need to do is stick it out through the plot twist.

Artwork

I never meant for you to see these scars.

Did my best to keep you at arm's length,

Not realizing my heart was already on my sleeve.

I keep it next to an unfinished tattoo of you

Because I rely on my regrets for everything I do.

Lately, I feel I need to spend more time with those imperfections,

So I keep adding artwork to this collection.

Feeling Feelings

If emotions are best when felt,

Then you'll understand my surprise,

In never being taught to read Braille.

21 Questions

Why does it seem that my milestones are magnets for death?

Is it my hue?

My roots?

Are you frightened by the depth of my origin story?

Why does the melanin in my knowledge cause you so much angst?

Why is it so hard for you when I take back my rightful place?

Why are you so prepared to document my pain?

But so absent-minded when we say from whence it came?

Why does my voice hide from every eulogy?

Why is it that tears always make it clearer who's kin to me?

How did we confuse love with standardless viewership?

How did I follow this marathon for so long but always forget to get in tune with it?

Once the feeling's gone can it be restored?

If it never leaves did you have to die for it?

If tomorrow comes and I'm still in a daze will you forgive me?

If I stumble under the new weight will you be with me?

Can you forgive me if I don't hold the torch as high?

If I don't finish the race as quick?

If I stop crying too soon?

If I run out of questions?

Caution Tape

I swore I'd never make a woman cry after I heard my mother shed

tears on her anniversary.

This is what happens when love outlives the loved.

This is why I swore I'd hate it.

But love and hate are forever connected,

Two sides of one coin subject to perspective.

I think it's why I cried when I saw love leave,

I knew it was her but I couldn't stand to make her bleed.

Then somehow,

Years and tears later,

I saw you.

In the dark with my eyes closed.

Your presence was the song that led my soul back to the world.

This is why we were created,

To deny this is unforgivable hatred.

So when I say I love you on this day,

Understand I don't say it lightly.

I know all too well that a heart isn't shatter proof,

And not enough of us tread lightly.

But if I have to spend every breath I have left tiptoeing around myself,

I promise to hold you gently.

Because you taught me about love,

Which means you taught me about God,

Which means you taught me about purpose,

Which means our spirits are forever intertwined,

And the caution is worth it.

Late Registration

When my brother was killed and I didn't say anything,
I realized I didn't know how to grieve.
I'm not sure where I was when they taught that.

When my mother's calls felt more burden than privilege,
I realized I didn't know how to be loved.
I'm not sure where I was when they taught that.

When my Granny died and I started calling to her spirit more than I
ever called her house,
I realized I didn't know how to be in a family.
I'm not sure where I was when they taught that.

When inspiration hit and I covered the wound in comfortable,
I realized I didn't know how to be more.
I'm not sure where I was when they taught that.

When I pulled up to the class a bit late,
I wasn't sure where I was...but I hope they're still teaching.

A Lone Wolf's Love Story Pt. 3

The day the Omega wolf decides enough is enough is always a
violent one.
It knows the pack depends on its silence,
On its acceptance of it all.
It knows that it must Atlas this family secret to atone for the way things
are,
Because that's just the way things are.
But fangs are fangs,
And wolves are wolves.
So if the day comes that the Omega shrugs its shoulders and decides
that this family will have this discussion,
It has already prepared for the bloodshed.
Know that after this things will never be the same.
Something will die here.

For a time,

Brutality was the only adjective I had for honesty.

The truth was a dagger that I kept at hand,

Ready and waiting to puncture the tension between tranquility and
chaos,

Covered in the ashes of everything I'd learned to sweep under the rug.

And I know I should be cautious with this weaponry,

But we don't own this house,

So I don't care if I leave stains on these floors.

PEMDAS

The most vivid memories I have of being told I was loved as a child all came after whoopings.

I know there were other moments when the emphasis was made,

But those are the ones that stand out.

Almost like the words were more pronounced because of the pain they followed,

Or the rage that birthed that pain,

Or the fear that justified that rage.

I wonder whose Aunt Sally excused that order of operations.

Love Language

I struggle with being loved.

Not because I don't deserve it,

I just searched long enough to know what it will cost,

And it's hard to find a way to ask this much of you.

Everything I'm Not

I am not a poet.
I can't be.
My words don't come together to fit the bill.
Still I spend my free time searching for ways to expand my vocabulary
so that your beauty can be explained.

I am not a lover.
I can't comprehend the action.
I've been on the defensive too long to learn that skill.
Yet I've spent my last dime on the tools needed to bring down the
walls I've built around my heart so you can hold it.

I am not a glass maker.
But I spend my nights wishing your reflection could show you how you
appear in my thoughts,
And hope that just once I can make it through the nightmares that
have fort knoxed my dreams of us and get a glimpse of my desires.
I wish I could tell you the words that my heart thinks when you reach
my thoughts.
I wish I could show you the light my spirit wears when you cross my
path.
I wish I could shatter the facade that separates me from us.

But I am not a poet.
I am not a lover.
I am not a glass maker.

These are words I cannot say because my soul is too burdened to be free.

So I stare at the ocean and pray you see what I see,

But never have to feel what I feel.

I send you my heart disguised as a smile that I hope you wear forever.

I fill every room we share with laughter so you only have happy thoughts of me.

With each hug we share I take your pain because you don't deserve it,

And I leave you with all the joy that was meant for you and I and us.

That way each day you have will be better than the last.

And each story you tell of me will make you forget that we can't last.

Then you won't be sad on the day I have to move on.

Then I will never have to apologize for not sharing this before you read it in a poem.

The Mantle

As a kid, I used to love spending the weekends stretched out on the bed next to my mom watching TV.

There always seemed to be a marathon of one of her favorite shows.

Law & Order

Columbo

In the Heat of the Night

Perry Mason

All filled with rules I didn't quite understand, but I loved that time.

She used to tell me I looked like my father.

I laid the same way he did.

I can't remember if she told me that with awe or devastation.

I can't remember if I ever checked.

When I moved out, I took a portrait of the two of them.

It sits on my mantle the same way she used to have it.

These days I spend my weekends under that picture hoping I can feel his presence while I watch my favorite shows.

Trying to remember what used to come natural when my head meets my pillow,

Hoping my father isn't somewhere disappointed that I've never been able to see his reflection when I look in the mirror

Or the window

Or the ocean.

Or any of the hundreds of places that everyone that knows him is so easily able to find him in this unfinished statue of me.

I assume I've always searched for him.

I just pray the journey doesn't end in the creation of a destiny where I leave my future seed with the memory of an absentee vote of confidence.

And I struggle to understand how I learned to value the weight of that ballot

Over the woman who shed tears in the footsteps of a ghost to always make sure I made it to the polls.

Thinking Out Loud

She asked why I don't write poems like I used to.

I told her I've run out of ways to avoid saying her name in metaphors.

I told her every word I wrote was addressed to her and I'm tired of burning the envelopes.

I told her I've run out of details to describe anything as beautiful as her,

That my imagination can't create anything more exquisite than her walk,

That the earth doesn't have a sound more soothing than when I hear her talk.

I told her that I loved her before I ever saw her.

That God paired our souls before he made the world

And only separated us at birth so he could enjoy our journey back to each other.

I told her...

She asked why I don't write poems like I used to.

I told her nothing.

I just shrugged.

I wish I wasn't in my own head so much.

Focus

Let's get lost on the road less traveled,

Find love in the air.

Prepare for the best,

Expect to see each other there.

They say a mind is a terrible thing to waste,

But as long as you're on mine I don't care about the other space.

Depression, in my own words

I spent today wondering what was worse.

That I keep a list of the blessings I've cost myself,

Or that I already know which wall I'm going to fill up next.

We're Here Now

For some reason, I have the hardest time remembering when I met
people.
It's almost like I wake up one day and here they are.
Important.
Present.
As if they'd always been there.
So you'll understand my confusion the day I realized that my sadness
had become one of my closest friends.
A sibling,
Conjoined to my reflection,
But hiding in the shadows of my potential.
I didn't know it mattered so much.
Didn't realize how long I'd let it guide me.
And it's not in my nature to end tours early,
You might as well get your money's worth.

No Publishing

By the 3rd grade, I knew I was a writer.

By the 5th grade, I hated every story I'd ever told.

I think it was the characters.

I loved them too much to let them go,

But everything is a story to share.

Maybe it was the lessons they taught,

Always on time but never enough,

Real life never ended with the fairy tale.

Perhaps it was too painful

To watch them go through the hurt,

The devil is always in the details.

To be honest, I just hated sharing.

The stories were like my deepest secrets,

And I always knew my spirit was uncomfortable in big crowds.

By the 3rd grade, I knew I was a writer.

By the 5th grade, I hated every story I'd ever told.

By now I've built a house on Writers Block,

Hoping I never find a pen,

So I can have a reason to blame my stories never getting out on not having publishing.

Growing Pains

When you grew up this close to your pain,

Healing feels like losing the closest of friends.

A Lone Wolf's Love Story Pt. 4

A wolf's howl is believed to happen for 1 of 3 reasons,

To mark a territory,

To find a pack it's lost,

Or to establish relationships.

Then the seasons change…

And each of those reasons becomes a reason for silence.

When the cubs are born, marking its territory could signal to predators where their vulnerabilities lie.

When gone from the pack too long, noise is a beacon that invites the enemy's swarm.

When the pack reaches hunting age,

And roles have been established,

Not everyone is worthy of your voice.

These were the examples used to dictionary my definition of love.

A fickle thing constantly swaying with the wind.

A moment, as clear as an eclipse but lost in the dark.

You'll know it when you see it they said,

I should've asked what to do next.

<u>**Get The Picture**</u>

A blind man once asked me,

Could I imagine what it was like to go blind and still be afraid of the dark?

I asked him if it was similar to being a Black man that's afraid of dying.

Not death itself but the process,

The anticipation.

The constant wondering if that's the reaper you hear around the corner

Waiting.

Having internalized that you'd be dead by 25,

And spending your 24th birthday wondering if next year your mother will spend this day inside,

Or turning 26 and waiting for someone to collect on this borrowed time.

Living a long life of looking over your shoulder,

And being told to be strong as you're strapped to another boulder.

Getting used to appreciating your nightmares simply because they end,

Getting used to avoiding people simply so they don't have to lose another friend.

I told him I couldn't say for sure if I knew what it was like,

But I wouldn't wish this on anyone so I hope we aren't alike.

He said, "Yeah, facing your fears can be tough.

But when we make it through, you always know you gave enough."

Siren Song Pt. 2

When the Greeks wrote of the Sirens,

They often differed on their appearance.

But it's their song that always survives this literary game of telephone.

Equal parts beautiful and sad.

A tragic song of temptation.

Yet no one knows what they actually said.

I shudder to think how much history men have altered because we

didn't listen first.

Broken Conversations

A woman told me,
Lying will direct your life,
If you lie to you.

I stared in reply,
What we had was almost great,
Lesson learned too late.

Love tried to tell me,
It's not better to have lost,
But okay to try.

I stared in reply,
My heart likes to sabotage,
My brain, it complies.

A better me said,
Stop ruining your chances,
Love is life's lock picked.

I stared in reply,
Love was never the problem,
The struggles in fall.

Aisle 6

I learned to love the same way I learned to shop with my mother,

Silently staring with my hands by my side,

Imagining the possibilities.

Trying not to embarrass anyone.

But if the eye is the window to the soul,

I pray you can see how my essence honors you.

And perhaps, when you remember these days,

You'll forgive me for always finding you when my pockets were empty.

Black Sheep

I don't know how you love me,
Or how to show you I feel the same.
My words ring hollow,
Sleep deprived in a headless world of endless pain,
Put on display at family dinners and holidays.

I'd go to battle for your name from here to Heaven's gates,
But face to face I don't have much to say.
I prefer to be alone
And give my best updates through Facebook since I don't ever use
the phone.

I won't bother with an apology because I've been this way forever,
And to be honest I thought by now you'd learn to take it better,
Though I can't really fault you for hoping that I'd change my ledger.
Maybe one day we can find a happy medium and bring the good
times back,
Too bad I've gotten used to being the sheep in black.

Snapshot

If a picture is worth a thousand words,

I hope you never see me working on these negatives.

A lifetime's worth of good memories,

I couldn't find the time to develop.

Just know that I see them.

Replay the scenes in my head.

Wishing one day you'll wander back into the darkroom

Turn on the lights and ruin everything I never said,

So we can start fresh from the click.

Balancing Act

I was still learning to ride a bike when I had my 1st growth spurt.

I remember how embarrassed I was to topple over every block,

So I convinced myself it'd be easier to rollerblade instead.

I have yet to pick a bike back up.

I was still learning to hear my heart when I had my 1st introduction to love.

I remember how embarrassed I was to see my words stumble into silence,

So I convinced myself it'd be easier to be alone instead.

I have yet to pick a love back up.

How ironic that I always find balance in my falls.

At The End of it All

When I was a kid, I tattooed my grandmother's house with a nail file.
I was 9.
My mother and I had just moved to California and were staying with her.
I moved my mattress to the side and wrote,
"I hate it here" on the bedroom wall.
They found it.
In response to that and what I'm sure was a top 3 all-time attitude that I was displaying, my mother asked me if I wanted to leave.
She gave me an out.
I could go back to Texas and live with my grandparents.
I'm not sure I've ever been closer to her pain than in that moment.
I told her I'd stay.
I told myself I broke her.
That my emotions were her kryptonite and how dare I try to kill Superman.
That was the day I started digging.
Determined to bury that part of me beneath the deepest oceans where I could never hear its screams.
Years later,
The world shifts.
Black men are encouraged to feel their emotions and my time capsule shakes lose.
It's heavier than I remember.
Filled with things I never meant to hide.
Decisions I barely recall.
Mistakes that I've built monuments of.

And nobody to blame because 9 year olds need their superheroes.

I'm not sure healing is for me.

Not convinced that taking the bandages off of my mummified heart is worth stopping life's train,

But I already opened the time capsule.

I put the shovel back in the shed.

I told the child in me that he didn't have to protect us anymore.

And I've seen far too much to think disaster won't come here again.